MW01201996

Transgender Confusion

A Biblically Based Q & A for Families

Help 4 Families

Copyright © 2016 Denise Shick
Help4Families Press
PMB 156 378 Diederich Blvd.
Ashland, KY 41101

www.help4families.org
help4families2004@yahoo.com
All rights reserved.
ISBN-13: 978-1518652608
ISBN-10: 1518652603

Dedication

To each family that faces one of the most challenging situations in life: gender confusion or transgenderism. For "God is our refuge and strength, a very present help in trouble."
Psalm 46:1 (ESV)

Disclaimer

About Denise Shick and *Help 4 Families*

Denise Shick is the founder and executive director of *Help 4 Families*. *Help 4 Families* is a nonprofit Christian ministry dedicated to offering encouragement and resources for those who struggle with gender confusion and their friends, families, and communities.

Denise has worked with families of gender-confused loved ones since 2004.

She diligently works alongside church leaders to bring understanding of the emotional and spiritual confusion that occurs when a loved one has gender confusion. She has led church-based support groups for people with sexual addictions.

She is the author of *My Daddy's Secret*, *When Hope Seems Lost,* and *Understanding Gender Confusion: A Faith-Based Perspective* and co-author of *Dangerous Affirmations*. She is a nationally recognized speaker and has been interviewed on several Christian radio and Christian television programs.

Trust in the lord with all your heart,

and do not lean on your own understanding.

PROVERBS 3:5 (ESV)

CONTENTS

Introduction

My purpose in writing this resource is to discuss both the issues that surround families touched by transgenderism and the difficult decisions those families must make. This has been one of the most difficult resources I have written, because I want to address the issues as biblically as I can while also respecting the sensitive circumstances and challenges these families face.

Ten years ago, few had ever heard the term *transgender*. When I was a child, virtually no one had heard the term. Oh, how things have changed in less than one generation. These days you cannot watch or read the news without hearing a story of this rapidly escalating movement in which truth and fantasy have become synonymous and lives are destroyed daily. Yet, in spite of all the publicity, most people are unaware of the damage the entire family suffers when a loved one falls under the spell of an impression that he or she was born in the wrong body.

The Bible reveals that *the LORD God made a woman from the rib he had taken out of the man, and he brought her to the man* (Genesis 2:22 NIV). God made man and woman, each distinctively and purposefully, but our culture has largely rejected even the concept of a God. And, because of that rejection, our culture has also rejected the sacredness of a person's God-given gender. The serpent's ancient fabrication in Genesis 3:4—*You will not certainly die* —echoes through our popular media, clinics, and hospital hallways. But with each transgender makeover, one of God's creations does die, only to be resurrected in a form foreign to the Creator's design for that unique individual.

I hope this resource will answer some of the difficult questions many ask. The real-life situations that strugglers and their families face are challenging. Unfortunately, both the struggler and the family can become discouraged and give up because of the frustration and despair they face day in and day out. But there is hope, and that hope lies within God's grace and His ability to heal gender brokenness.

PART 1
Science & Feelings

What Is Transgenderism?

Transgenderism is a condition in which a person feels inadequate and is distressed in his or her God-given gender. The person has strong, persistent desires to look like and become the opposite gender. Many say they prayed and prayed, but still they woke up in the morning, pulled back their bedcovers, and disappointingly saw that they still had the same body parts they had before going to sleep. The desire to be the other gender are intense and seem undeniable.

Their distress can seem unbearable at times, especially for the female-to-male when her menstrual cycle appears, or for the male-to-female when he realizes the only way to begin to pass as a female is to wear heavy makeup.

Girls are more inclined to reject their gender role in societies where women are marginalized and devalued. Girls are also more inclined toward cross-gender wishes because of the belief that men are more highly valued or esteemed. Daughters who witness their mother being repeatedly verbally and/or physically abused by males may begin to see themselves as little more than an object that serves no purpose other than to please men. This creates fear of womanhood, which they see as a weakness that makes them a potential object of abuse.

4

Boys may reject their own masculinity because of negative, abusive, and weak role models. It is also possible that overbearing and abusive male role models could cause a boy to run from his masculinity. They experience feelings of discomfort with the thought of growing up to become a man. Boys who do not enjoy or do not excel at common male activities, such as sports, may develop a negative self-image. They may also accept the idea that they are girly or sissy because of repeated teasing or ostracism at school or at home by family members. The absence of opposite-sex role models for both boys and girls can also result in a degree of uncertainty and insecurity about their own gender identity, as well as avoidance of or lack of comfort with the same sex. A large number of people who struggle with gender non-conformity often struggle with transgenderism.

The absence of a male role model may leave boys feeling awkward among same-sex peers. Later, as men, they may be inadequately prepared for the role of husband and father, leading to feelings of failure and discomfort in the male role. Mentally disturbed or absent mothers can likewise leave girls feeling inadequate and unacceptable in their gender role. Daughters of divorced or abandoned mothers may step in to fill the role of the absent father, often being praised by their mothers for their "masculine" traits.

Gender confusion and same-sex attraction can lead to transsexualism when there are highly negative attitudes toward homosexuality. In this case, the cross-gender identity is used to justify the same-sex attraction as being heterosexual and therefore acceptable to themselves and others. In severe cases, confusion about gender can arise out of adolescent adjustment disorders, or from part of a more generalized identity confusion in which questions such as *Who am I?* and *Where do I fit in?* encompass the question of *What gender am I?*

When individuals have suffered such a breakdown in their psychosexual development, they end up erotically idolizing (cannibalizing) the other sex, thinking that being a member of that gender would be the appropriate medicinal agent to cure the intense emotional pain.

Generally, cross-gender feelings and behaviors are not persistent throughout life; rather, they manifest as a coping mechanism during stressful life events. Treatment of transsexualism involves the resolution of the underlying contributing factors. Initially, explorative therapy is valuable in order to obtain relevant history and to identify any co-morbid psychopathology.

Some people with a background of severe abuse, especially sexual abuse, may be treated or referred for treatment for that abuse. Others, with personality disorders, dissociative disorders, and other psychopathology can likewise undergo treatment for those disorders. In cases where gender-identity disorders exist in the context of broader identity problems or issues, the patient may benefit from exploring issues related to self-identity within therapy. To facilitate therapy, psychotropic medications may be prescribed during treatment.

Socially, persons with gender-identity disorders will benefit from associations with healthy male and female role models, wherein any wrong or inappropriate ideas they hold about sex-roles can be challenged and corrected.

The greatest barrier to treatment lies with the patients who refuse to accept any responsibility for their behavior(s) and are unwilling to question the origin of their condition, explore its causes or development, entertain thoughts of change, or make any attempt to change.

Sadly, another barrier to proper help is society's affirmation of and acquiescence to a person who wishes to be the other gender. This acceptance has led to authorities allowing very young people who are gender-confused to affirm their feelings and start treatment to change, often well before they have reached maturity and possibly before they have reached puberty.

Those who want to provide intervention to help individuals identify the root causes and to heal from their gender confusion are often marginalized and threatened with professional or legal sanctions. Some movements now seek to ban therapies that could help individuals heal from their gender confusion.

Ultimately, people who identify as transgender suffer from the same problem we all face: we live in a fallen world. We all must choose between right and wrong; we all wrestle with things we do not like about ourselves. We all struggle with sin. Even the apostle Paul found himself doing what he did not want to do (Romans 7:14-25). It is our response, not our struggle, that matters. We can attempt to justify our wrong feelings, desires, and actions, or we can turn to God through His Son, Jesus Christ, and allow Him to transform us into the person

God created us to be, including, in the case of transsexuals, bringing them back to gender wholeness.

What Is the Difference between Homosexuality and Transsexuality?

This is a common question, and one that deserves to be answered frankly. Individuals who struggle with same-sex attraction are more than likely to have developed relational issues with their same sex-parent and their gender peers.

While a person who struggles with same-sex attraction has developed emotional issues with the same-sex parent, it is also likely there are issues with the opposite-sex parent in one form or another. Either real or perceived judgments from parents or peers can cause same-sex attracted individuals to struggle in their masculinity or femininity. When there is a lack of validation of their masculinity or femininity, they seek to fill it from another source.

The person carries a deep-seated envy of that same-sex parent or person. The person has same-sex relational and emotional disconnections and does not usually desire to be seen and accepted as a member to the opposite sex. These individuals are trying to connect with a member of the same sex in order to feel complete. It is an attempt to repair the emotional damage that was done early in life (Moberly). Transsexual behavior is a response to a growing discontent with having to live as a member of their God-designed, natural-born gender.

A male who identifies as being transgender remains attached emotionally, if not literally, to mom's soft and safe world. He has a deep-seated envy of girls; he strongly desires to be like his mother and, in a sense, "own" her femininity. The female is unattached to her mother's world and feels that by becoming a man, she will be able to control her destiny. She may vow that in becoming a man, no man will ever hurt her again. She has detached herself from her femininity.

Various reasons can motivate a person to step out of maleness or femaleness and choose the opposite gender identity. The point is, both the males and females who choose this drastic change have rejected their God-given gender because of their unhappiness, disappointment, and resentment. A break has occurred between their heart and soul.

Ultimately, we must recognize this tear in the human soul. For too long, the image of manhood in our culture has been corrupted by the model of one primarily oriented toward seeking. The seeker's focus, or lifestyle orientation, tends to reflect his own self-serving human nature instead of God's image or desire for him.

Is a Person Born This Way?

No studies have proved that anyone has been born transgender. No matter how many cosmetic surgeries and hormones one has ingested, his or her biology, (sex chromosomes), neurology, and genetic composition (DNA) remains unchangeable. The person's reproductive system is the one he or she was born with. The born-that-way theories are nothing more than propaganda purported by advocates who want to gain public sympathy and approval.

Physicians have the ability to transform male genitals into genitals that appear female, but they are not able to change men into women and women into men. This is a biological fact. The person may resemble the opposite gender, and even pass as one of the opposite gender due to the cosmetic surgeries and hormones, but the change is "reality" only within that person's confused thoughts.

The answers are different for each person who has an inner identity struggle. However, many have come to understand that the seeds of their confusion were planted through their experiences, such as an unexpected trauma, loss, family dysfunction, or sexual abuse. The person is looking for an escape route in order to run from their pain and turmoil. It is vital for the hurting to feel loved and valued by the One who created them. Through the love of Christ and others, the healing journey begins.

Biblical Truth: As Christians, we resist the idea that we are in charge of our destiny. We acknowledge that, ultimately, God is. *The mind of man plans his way, but the LORD directs his steps* (Proverbs 16:9 NASB). We have forgotten that our gender is a key element of our identity, given to, but not made by, us. Genesis 1:27 emphasizes that God created basic and clear differences between men and women, and Psalm 139:13 says, *For you [God] created my inmost being; you knit me together in my mother's womb* (NIV).

Can Gender Really Be Changed?

A person seeking to change his or her gender feels little to no value in who they are as God's creation. The reflection of how one feels should be addressed in a serious manner, for it is a serious issue. The person is not only acting in a way that can destroy his or her physical and mental health, but also rebelling against the Creator who formed male and female distinctions.

The issues behind one's gender identity are personal and painful for those who struggle and for their loved ones. Many former transgender people admit that they experienced deep emotional wounds and/or rejection that caused the inner turmoil with their God-given gender. Often it is caused by psychological and sociological factors. But the plain truth is that no one can really change his or her gender.

The attempt to do so is made through surgical alternation of human tissue to bring the superficial, external anatomical appearance into some sense of congruity with the inward perceptions of what has become an individual's sense of reality.

But the result is little more than an illusion. In reality, most people who identify as being transgender have to think about how to act, walk, and present themselves as the opposite gender. Their fantasies begin to take control, and they demonstrate an obsessiveness to present and to be approved as the opposite gender. As others affirm the false identity, the false beliefs about that gender gain ground.

If someone has his foot in freshly poured cement, and the cement begins to dry, what happens? The person tries and tries to get his foot out of the cement by shaking his leg and pulling with all his strength.

The cement thickens, and with each passing minute, it becomes more difficult for the person to get free.

Biblical Truth: If your loved ones struggles with transgenderism, they need to learn and accept that they cannot really change their gender; this is not the solution. However, they *can* change their desire to be someone else, but only with God's help. The Spirit of God is in the business of changing His people and their hearts: *Thieves nor the greedy nor drunkards nor slanderers nor swindlers will inherit the kingdom of God. And that is what some of you were. But you were washed, you were sanctified, you were justified in the name of the Lord Jesus Christ and by the Spirit of our God* (1 Corinthians 6:10-11 NIV). *The LORD is near to the heartbroken and He saves those who are crushed in spirit (contrite in heart, truly sorry for their sin)* (Psalm 34:18 AMP).

Is Gender Confusion Treatable?

Yes! The earlier the treatment is offered, the better one's outcome is likely to be in coming to terms with and embracing his or her God-given gender. Dr. Marc S. Dillworth, PhD, uses a treatment model that encourages father/son bonding. Fathers need to beware of demonstrating an attitude of criticism toward their sons. The idea is to turn the son back through positive interactions that create the attentiveness and affirmation the son needs.

Recognize the father's importance. If the father's personality is not strong or inviting enough to draw forth from his son his inherent masculinity, the son can easily choose not to leave his mother's nurturing presence. Because the mother is present and accessible, the boy's most-focused emotion says, "Let go of me, Mom!" But his more primal cry is, "Come and get me, Dad!" A boy's over-bonding with the mother, therefore, reflects a weak, abusive, or absent father.

Too much mothering can create an unhealthy attachment for the son. The mother needs to cut the apron strings and nudge her son toward his father. The son would benefit from the mother affirming the father's masculinity. This can be difficult, of course, if the father is abusive in any way.

Rather than telling a son, "Boys your age don't play with dolls; you can play with the GI Joe," use positive encouragement for gender-appropriate behavior. And, finally, encourage the child to have and play with same-sex friends and activities (Dillworth). Ultimately, children need to be praised, not torn down.

Girls need to have a healthy perspective of womanhood; they need to see it as a safe and admirable existence. Most girls face difficult times of being judged by their peers. Can she fit in? Is she pretty enough? Does she wear the right clothes? Does her family have the right connections in the community?

A girl might even be rejected if the leader of the in-group perceives her to be a threat because she is seen as being too pretty or too privileged. She also has to work her way through the dating gauntlet.

Will boys think she is pretty enough to warrant their attention? How should she behave around them?

In addition to all those concerns, there is the father factor—or, all too often, the missing-father factor. To be emotionally healthy, a girl needs a father who will support her and display healthy affection toward her. Girls who do not receive such affirmation often devalue themselves.

Another problem is the power of suggestion. Whether through peers or media influences, a girl may come to believe that taking on a different identity could be the best way to escape her anxiety. Transsexuality is a pathway in which the anxiety finds a release that was ultimately formed from an emotional unmet need from childhood wounds.

Biblical Truth: As a parent, use positive reinforcement. It is a better investment to build a child up than to tear a child down. God's Word tells us we are to *encourage one another and build each other up* (1 Thessalonians 5:11 NIV). *Fathers, don't exasperate your children by coming down hard on them. Take them by the hand and lead them in the way of the Master* (Ephesians 6:4 MSG). *And above all these put on love, which binds everything together in perfect harmony* (Colossians 3:14 ESV).

But Aren't Their Brains Different?

This question was addressed in a recent paper by Savic and Arver. "The authors found that the brains in their study group were *not feminised.* There was no evidence for female brains in a male body; the brains were male-typical" (Whitehead & Hutt, emphasis added).

This is contrary to many of the previous research studies on mixed groups, but the study is thorough. Savic and Arver also found differences in the brains of their study-group participants that were not found in either heterosexual male or heterosexual female brains. These regions have been identified as those possibly associated with bodily self-perception. (They are also enlarged in those who do a lot of meditation, focusing partly on body state.)

The authors say this is a "highly speculative" interpretation, but it is possible they are actually underestimating how much support it has. It is very clear that repeated patterns of mental exercise alone—as seen, for example, in navigation (London taxi drivers) and Internet addiction (Whitehead & Hutt)—changes significantly the microstructure of the brain. Thinking, particularly repeated thinking, changes brain microstructure (Whitehead & Hutt). The differences found in the brain studies could also be caused by hormonal medications—differences that may not have been present prior to the chemical manipulation.

According to Paul McHugh, professor of psychiatry at Johns Hopkins, "It is a disorder of the mind. Not a disorder of the body" (McHugh). Another psychiatrist, Rick Fitzgibbons, describes gender dysphoria as "a fixed false belief of a serious thinking disorder, specifically a delusion" (Fitzgibbons).

Even when people have had sex-reassignment surgery, and they assume they have become what they sought to be, the reality is that only the outside changes. The person is clinging to a false perception. Billie Sue, a post-operative male-to-female transsexual, states:

> My hatred for being a man became the turning point for my becoming a transsexual. Standing naked in front of a mirror, I hated my male organs, which my therapist affirmed as real evidence that proved I was truly a transsexual. As we absorb estrogen, our emotions do change, and many times we find men becoming more attractive to us, but while we are in that state before hormone therapy, many of us did indeed hate men. This hatred is often resolved by taking female hormones. But the underlying reason I was transsexual was because of my hatred for men, and the hatred for my own body, as well as the role I'd have to play as a man.

James confesses to forcing others to accept his new identity in his attempt to bring others (including his former wife), into his fantasy. "I silently felt accepted as a woman when I passed as a woman, but in the process I threatened the core of my being."

Biblical Truth: God did not create males or females to feel trapped in the body He gave them. God created male and female in His own image. *In the image of God he created them; male and female he created them* (Genesis 1:27 NIV). Sometimes we forget that we live in a fallen world where our perception of truth becomes deluded.

PART 2
Family Questions & Answers

Your Loved One Just Said He or She Is Transgender. What Can You Do?

Hearing this dramatic identification can be painful. It usually blindsides us "especially when the news relates to someone we love and care about very much. Nehemiah grieved over the report of hardships faced by his people, his spiritual family, who had lost everything dear to them and were living 'in great trouble and disgrace'" (Wagstaff). And we are no different from Nehemiah when facing this situation in our family.

The world does not comprehend the danger of the transgender movement, and of causing *one of these little ones—those who believe in [Jesus]—to stumble* (Matthew 18:6 NIV). If your child is young and shows signs of gender dysphoria, seek professional help through a therapist who is aligned with your beliefs as soon as possible.

A good therapist will be able to provide you with tools for communicating with your child and addressing his or her gender confusion. Often, this means addressing your relationship with your child and how that relationship may need to be strengthened through constructive modeling.

If your loved one who identifies as transgender is an adult, you will face a period of denial and deep grief. Your dreams for your loved one have gone astray (at least at this time). But remember that Christ loves your loved one far more than you do. That might seem impossible. However, when you come to terms with this deep truth, you will learn to let go and let God deal with the situation. Cry out to God in your crisis. You need to see the situation as God does; more than likely, it is an opportunity to draw closer to Him.

This is a journey on which you must learn to trust the Lord with all your heart. When you take your eyes off Jesus, you start to trust your own actions. But only God can handle this. *Do not be wise in your own eyes* (Proverbs 3:7 NIV).

Who are *you*? Yes, your loved one has a broken view of his or her identity, but it is equally important to know who you are, and who God says you are in Him. In Acts 15, the apostle James said, *"Simon has described to us how God first intervened to choose a people for his name from the Gentiles. The words of the prophets are in agreement with this, as it is written: 'After this I will return and rebuild David's fallen tent. Its ruins I will rebuild'"* (vv. 14-16 NIV).

God will work within you to bring the restoration you seek. Does this happen instantly? More than likely, no. Your healing will come, but it will be a process, as you must face reality to deal with your true feelings and hurts. The hurt you feel is deep; the journey is difficult. God has a work to do within you, not just within your loved one. Colossians 2:10 says, *And in Him you have been made complete* (NASB).

Biblical Truth: We have help in heart-wrenching times like this. Scripture reminds us that *the LORD is a refuge for the oppressed, a* *stronghold in times of trouble* (Psalm 9:9 NIV). Though you may feel alone, with nowhere to run, remember that *the name of the LORD is a fortified tower; the righteous run to it and are safe* (Proverbs 18:10 NIV).

How Do I Tell My Family Members?

No one should feel pressured to share information with their family and friends. Many times the person experiencing this journey will go through periods of denial, grief, guilt, anger, and forgiveness. The time for sharing the news with your family and friends will come when you are ready emotionally.

When you do tell your family and friends, you can have the assurance that God is your rock. Cling to Him, and He will make you strong where you are weak. *Don't fret or worry. Instead of worrying, pray. Let petitions and praises shape your worries into prayers, letting God know your concerns. Before you know it, a sense of God's wholeness, everything coming together for good, will come and settle you down. It's wonderful what happens when Christ displaces worry at the center of your life* (Philippians 4:6-7 MSG).

Indeed, God's peace will enable you to climb out of your despair and breathe the air He provides so you can speak to your family and friends about what you are facing. Help 4 Families Ministry is here to walk alongside you by providing an open-handed and biblical approach.

You cannot control how other family members and friends will respond. Regardless of how others react, know that God is there with you. As your relationship with Him becomes deeper, your healing will come. God will be walking this path with you, so communicate with Him through prayer. *Then you will call on me and come and pray to me, and I will listen to you* (Jeremiah 29:12 NIV).

Biblical Truth: The psalmist wrote, *But as for me, it is good to be near God. I have made the Sovereign LORD my refuge* (Psalm 73:28 NIV). God says, *"Call to me and I will answer you and tell you great and unsearchable things you do not know"* (Jeremiah 33:3 NIV)

How Can Grandparents Help?

I often hear from grandparents whose hearts are broken over a grandchild declaring himself or herself to be transgender. In a sense, their pain is doubled. They grieve not only over their grandchild's wayward choice, but their heart also aches for their child who is enduring this loss and pain. Sometimes a grandparent feels he or she was responsible for setting the family standards, and somehow that standard was lost. Grandparents, do not despair. Continue to live a life of integrity at home and in public; allow your grandchildren to witness Christ's love for them through your life. You can do this by actions as well as words, so never give up acting as Christ would act at all times. Never cease from lifting up your prayers for your grandchild and your child. Know that as your heart breaks, so does the Lord's.

Biblical Truth: *Even when I am old and gray, do not forsake me, my God, till I declare your power to the next generation, your might to* *all who are to come* (Psalm 71:18 NIV). *The righteous will flourish like a palm tree…. They will still bear fruit in old age; they will stay fresh and green, proclaiming, 'The LORD is upright; he is my Rock, and there is no wickedness in him'* (Psalm 92:12, 14-15 NIV).

Did Your Loved One Choose to Be Transgender?

No one would choose to "feel" they were the opposite gender. People do not always choose how they feel about themselves. But feelings can transfer over through personal experiences, hurts, and rejections, causing the person to seek escape. Sometimes psychological conditions need to be assessed.

Gender-reassignment surgery has become accepted and relatively common, leaving vulnerable people feeling that there is no other way for them to find peace. Despite this view, post-operative transgenders report a high level of stress and depression. Jesus Christ is the only One who can bring them peace, as He digs into their hearts and reveals the underlying issues from which they are running. Jeffrey, who gave his testimony at one of the Help 4 Families Hope Gathering conferences, said that while he was looking into a mirror, "God said, 'Honey, this isn't who you are.'" That was all it took for Jeffery to take his first steps on the road to healing. The enemy can use the power of suggestion, but God can use the power of truth.

No matter how difficult it may be, encourage and help your loved one to face the reality of his or her idolatry and self-centeredness, but mix the truth with ample portions of love, grace, patience, and forbearance. The most difficult challenge family and friends face is to avoid entering into the loved one's fantasy world, where he or she sees transitioning as the "true fix."

Praying for others is a privilege. It is also a crucial way you can combat the lies your loved one believes about himself or herself. If you do not pray and continue to be in prayer for your loved one, you are abandoning that person to the deception and stronghold that entraps him or her. Praying is an honest, humble, and personal way to reach out to God. Ask Him to help your loved one be open to His presence and healing.

Biblical Truth: God says, *"For I am the LORD, who heals you"* (Exodus 15:26 NIV). *This is what the LORD says: "Restrain your voice from weeping and your eyes from tears, for your work will be rewarded," declares the LORD. "They will return from the land of the enemy. So there is hope for your descendants," declares the LORD. "Your children will return to their own land"* (Jeremiah 31:16-17 NIV).

Noticing a Loved One Hiding Opposite-Gender Clothing under the Bed

Cross-dressing can turn into a compulsive and addictive behavior. If you notice your loved one hiding clothes or secretly dressing in clothing of the opposite gender, realize the dangers that are likely to develop from this type of behavior. The cycle can and often does start out as experimental, but it can go way beyond experimental after sexual or emotional release takes hold. When my father was stressed, he escaped and gained his emotional release through cross-dressing. Feelings can become a "need" that desires to be fed by an action. Once the brain receives this "food" for its euphoric release, it can take over someone's life.

By all means, no matter how difficult it may be, face the reality of what you see. Quite a few of us may choose to pray, "Please take the fear of the unknown from me, Lord Jesus. I place my fears in Your hands as I lay them down at Your altar. Help me, Lord, to face the truth. Amen."

Biblical Truth: How will you get past your fears? Paul wrote, *But he [the Lord] said to me, "My grace is sufficient for you, for my power is made perfect in weakness." Therefore I will boast all the more gladly about my weaknesses, so that Christ's power may rest on me* (2 Corinthians 12:9 NIV).

My Loved One Believes God Made A Mistake

You may not be able to change your loved one's belief that God made a mistake with his or her born gender. Rest in knowing that God will run after your loved one's heart. If you do not rest in this truth, you will wear yourself out before you finally get on your knees. The key is to get on your knees first. Through the Holy Spirit speaking into your loved one's heart in drawing him or her close to Him, he or she will see that *the LORD appeared to us in the past, saying: "I have loved you with an everlasting love; I have drawn you with unfailing kindness"* (Jeremiah 31:3 NIV).

Many times the Lord will use the actions of a stranger to correct your loved one's false belief that God made a mistake. One man spoke of the time he was in a women's restroom. An elderly lady came out and handed him a card with the name of a ministry leader on it. Then she said, "Honey, you need to talk to him." The elderly lady said nothing else, nor did she need to. She spoke with kindness and then left quietly. That was a life-changing moment for this man. Believeing God made a mistake could not be further from the truth. God is truth. It is the enemy, not God, who causes these inner conflicts.

Great is our LORD, and of great power: His understanding is infinite (Psalm 147:5 KJV). Numbers 23:19 reveals that *God is not a man, that he should lie; neither the son of man, that he should repent: hath he said, and shall he not do it? or hath he spoken, and shall he not make it good?* (KJV). God is not like us. He makes no mistakes, and He does not change His mind. God is the infinite power who brings to pass that which He has spoken. This is something that can easily be forgotten when we are in the midst of our painful journey.

Biblical Truth: In the end, we must recognize and respect that God is not like man, whose mistaken and sinful morality requires retribution. *God is light; in Him there is no darkness at all* (1 John 1:5 NIV). *The LORD is righteous in all His ways, and holy in all his works* (Psalm 145:17 KJV).

My Loved One Is Transitioning And Has Children. How Do We

Handle This?

You continue to love and relate to your loved one as you have in the past. Just because he or she identifies as being transgender does not mean you end your relationship, unless your loved one chooses to do so. Sure, this brings challenges you have not faced, and it may present new boundaries in the home and in your relationship. But remember, Christ did not back down from setting boundaries for His followers. We live within boundaries every day, whether those boundaries are from God, our employer, society, or in our relationships with family and friends. You do not have to apologize to your loved one for setting healthy boundaries for yourself and other family members.

In *Boundaries*, Dr. Henry Cloud and Dr. John Townsend make the following observations:

> We have many boundary problems because of relational fears. We are beset by fears of guilt, not being liked, loss of love, loss of connection, loss of approval, receiving anger, being known, and so on. Codependent, boundaryless people co-sign the note of life for the irresponsible person. Then they end up paying the bills—physically, emotionally, and spiritually—and the spendthrift continues out of control with no consequences. He continues to be loved, pampered, and treated nicely.
>
> Establishing boundaries helps codependent people stop interrupting the Law of Sowing and Reaping in their loved one's life. Boundaries force the person who is doing the sowing to also do the reaping.

Boundaries actually play an important role for us; they not only define us, but they also provide a way to preserve our soul, and sometimes our mental and emotional heath as well.

Through prayer, you will come to a place where you will be able to let go and let God! Be there for the children. You play a vital role by demonstrating a sense of security in your gender. You are also able to demonstrate relating to others of your own gender. These are simple concepts that children need to witness. Finally, pray with the children, expressing Jesus' presence with them. This will encourage them to call upon His name as they need Him.

Biblical Truth: *Do not be deceived: God cannot be mocked. A man reaps what he sows. Whoever sows to please their flesh, from the flesh will reap destruction; whoever sows to please the Spirit, from the Spirit will reap eternal life* (Galatians 6:7-8 NIV). *For every person will have to bear [with patience] his own burden [of faults and shortcomings for which he alone is responsible]* (Galatians 6:5 AMP).

My Loved One Asked Me to Pay for Hormone Therapy.
When a son or daughter specifically asks a parent to provide support by paying for hormone therapy, one must ask a few questions: What message am I sending by doing this? Will paying for this give me peace? Will other boundaries or belief systems be affected if I do this?

Let's tackle the first question first. What message will you send by paying for hormone therapy? Your loved one will likely believe that since you are paying for the hormones, you are supporting his or her actions at some level. Words are powerful, but our actions are at least as powerful as words.

The next question is, will paying for this give you peace? The chemicals used in the process do change one's appearance and voice. But those superficial changes are mere deceptions. The hormones (the deceiving agents) can cause potentially harmful complications and reactions. We should not expect to digest man-made chemicals without those drugs potentially interfering with the God-created body.

A few of the consequences that should be recognized as real possibilities are Type-II diabetes, increased high blood pressure, and other cardiovascular health isues. Also cancer risk is associated with hormonal therapies.

Some suggest that hormones are a "fix" on the pathway to gender transition, but this "fix" commonly causes mood swings, increased anger, and increased aggressiveness after starting androgen therapy (Israel & Tarver).

The confused person's skewed belief system can become stronger if you buy the hormones. In doing so, you are aiding the stronghold that controls your loved one. If I had bought my dad's hormones, I would have been embracing the false idea that he was a woman. I would also have kept him from seeing the truth, causing him to run right into the enemy's camp, and supporting his belief that God made a mistake when He created my dad.

This would not have given me peace, nor would it have secured the other boundaries I set with my dad. If I cave in on one boundary, the other boundaries may be weakened and become vulnerable.

Bible Truth: *This is what the LORD says—your Redeemer, who formed you in the womb. "I am the LORD, the Maker of all things, who* *stretches out the heavens, who spreads out the earth by myself"* (Isaiah 44:24 NIV). The Lord is the Creator of each and every one of us. That is the plain truth. Humans are not able to redefine their biological sex, no matter how hard anyone tries. *For in him[Christ] all things were created: things in heaven and on earth, visible and invisible, whether thrones or powers or rulers or authorities; all things have been created through him and for him* (Colossians 1:16 NIV).

Our Loved One Says He/She Is Transgender. He/She Is Living with a Person of the Same Gender. Does This Mean They Are a Gay Couple?

Such a relationship is not biblical. When partners were born of the same gender and one has had sex-reassignment surgery, the relationship is homosexual; it is a deceptive representation of a heterosexual relationship. It is then, in a sense, homosexual, even if the partners do not self-identify as gay or lesbian.

This is similar to the situation in which two transgendered people who were born of the opposite sex (one born male but transitioned to female and the other born female but transitioned to male) wish to marry and live as a genuine heterosexual couple. Either way, *evildoers and impostors will go from bad to worse, deceiving and being deceived* (2 Timothy 3:13 NIV). One who imposes on himself an opposite gender is simply deceived.

The situation obviously becomes further complicated as children are brought into such a scenario only to discover that Mom or Dad really is not of the sex they had been led to believe until that time. The complication is very difficult for all involved when a "mother" then desires to go back to living as a man, or a "father" as a woman. Although a loved one has decided at one point to transition, this does not mean it is impossible for God to reach deep down within a person's heart and soul to reach him or her.

As humans, we hunger to relate to God. At the same time, we also hunger to be sovereign over what we consider to be our domain. But only God can truly fill the hunger He placed within each of us.

Biblical Truth: *There is a way that seemeth right unto a man, but the end thereof are the ways of death* (Proverbs 16:25 KJV). *For he satisfies the longing soul, and the hungry soul he fills with good things* (Psalm 107:9 ESV).

Should You Allow Your Gender-Confused Loved One to Dress As He or She Wishes?

Sometimes well-meaning family members or friends will recommend that a wife, parent, or child of a gender-confused person endorse a loved one's self-perception. Such a view completely overlooks the Christian view that the Creator specifically and purposely designs each person's gender. Wives, parents, and children are often told they are selfish if they set boundaries such as the disapproval of a relative who wants to enter their home dressed as the opposite gender.

In such a scenario, the cross-dresser fails to consider the feelings of family members, many of whom simply "cannot go there." This does not mean those family members are bad; it means they are wise, as they recognize the emotional and spiritual darkness that can accompany such behaviors.

Overlooked in all the demands for tolerance and acceptance is the potential for emotional damage to family members who are pressured to applaud the sight of, for example, a son adorned in a dress and heels, wearing lipstick and mascara.

A mother will not forget a painful declaration from her son, and she will probably never be able to erase from her mind the startling visual image of the boy she gave birth to gliding into her living room dressed as a woman. This is equally difficult for a wife whose husband is transitioning. The man whom she has loved now appears as a woman. She cannot fight an illusion or the affair her husband is having with this illusion of a woman.

The focus typically is directed toward respecting the desires of the cross-dresser, but why should the sensitivities of the loved ones be ignored? The issue impacts not only the person who sees himself or herself as someone other than who he or she really is, but it also impacts all those involved—family members and other loved ones.

Boundaries are difficult. But when you are dealing with a loved one caught up in this type of struggle, the boundaries you set are both necessary for you and helpful for the person with the issue. It is your responsibility to take care of yourself.

Biblical Truth: There is nothing wrong with setting boundaries to protect oneself; doing so is the voice of wisdom speaking to your heart and soul. *The revelation of GOD is whole and pulls our lives together. The signposts of GOD are clear and point out the right road. The life-maps of GOD are right, showing the way to joy.... There's more: God's Word warns us of danger and directs us to hidden treasure. Otherwise, how will we find our way? Or know when we play the fool? Clean the slate, God, so we can start the day fresh! Keep me from stupid sins, from thinking I can take over your work; then I can start this day sun-washed, scrubbed clean of the grime of sin. These are the words in my mouth; these are what I chew on and pray. Accept them when I place them on the morning altar, O God, my Altar-Rock, God, Priest-of-My-Altar.* (Psalm 19:7-8; 11-14 MSG).

PART 3

When Jack Wants to Be Called Jill or Susie Wants to Be Called Sam

Names And Pronouns

Before we dive into this next section on our loved one wanting or demanding to be called a new name, and the accompanying pronoun issues, I ask that each of us stop and really think about how these issues developed. This answer is not the same for everyone. Some of you have a child in high school who has surrounded himself or herself with others (peers, teachers, support groups) who embrace his or her new identity. Many young people are surrounded by others outside their home who will teach them to embrace who they are.

Because of such influences, parents should do all they can to make a difference in the home and in their relationship with their child. Relationships with your children need to be your priority. As often as possible, sit with your child(ren) during mealtime. Choose to spend more time with your children and less time in front of the TV and on the computer or smartphone. Discover what your child likes to do, and do it with him or her. Moms, if your daughter likes to play a sport, go to her games. And dads, if your son likes to play the piano or dance, be there with him.

If you have found yourself in this place with a loved one—whether child, spouse, or parent—examine your heart to see if you may have intentionally or unintentionally supported your loved one's desire to transition. You need to support the person, but not the desire.

If you have not signaled your support—explicitly or implicitly—and are caught by surprise, you are not alone. Still, a look into past actions is helpful. For instance, did you allow cross-dressing in the home or in public? Did you give permission for the loved one to do this in the privacy of a bedroom or when no one else is home? If so, your loved one will likely expect you to move in the direction of affirmation, such as using the new name and its accompanying pronouns.

Biblical Truth: *The proverbs of Solomon, son of David, king of Israel: for gaining wisdom and instruction; for understanding words of insight; for receiving instruction in prudent behavior, doing what is right and just and fair; for giving prudence to those who are simple, knowledge and discretion to the young—let the wise listen and add to their learning, and let the discerning get guidance* (Proverbs 1:1-5 NIV). *But, speaking the truth in love, we are to grow up in all aspects into Him who is the head, even Christ* (Ephesians 4:15 NASB).

My Loved One Insists Our Family Use Preferred Pronouns.

What do we do? When people ask me this question, I share the experience I had with my dad. Even as I child, I sensed that if I referred to my dad as "her" or "she," I would be speaking lies into his heart. When people face this dilemma, remember that our ways often conflict with God's ways. If I had addressed my dad as Becky, or by female pronouns, I would have affirmed his choice. But 1 John 1:6 says, *If we say that we have fellowship with Him and yet walk in the darkness, we lie and do not practice the truth* (NASB). By giving into my dad's desire to be referred to as a woman, I would have practiced darkness rather than the truth. Remember, *there is no unrighteousness in Him [Jesus Christ]* (John 7:18 NASB).

Affirmation can be a slippery slope, an entryway into much more. "I'm only asking you to refer to me as____." Once this line has been crossed, the person's identification with a false self is affirmed. You have denied the fundamental truth of God's creation.

Denying your loved one's request to be referred to by his or her chosen identity may be the most difficult and heart-wrenching decision family and friends make. It must be covered in prayers for strength, for wisdom, and for our actions to honor God. It is difficult but necessary to *do your best to present yourself to God as one approved, a worker who has no need to be ashamed, rightly handling the word of truth* (2 Timothy 2:15 ESV).

When the truth is ignored in your home or in your relationship, there is little chance that your loved one will hear it anywhere else, almost certainly not in today's culture.

Reality must be based on who Christ says we are and who He is fashioning us to be in a daily relationship with Him. Our loved one's true identity will be found in Christ, not in some false feminine or masculine image of his or her imagination.

Consenting to the request to use a new name and different pronouns surrenders truth—a fundamental issue to God. *They exchanged the truth about God for a lie, and worshiped and served created things rather than the Creator* (Romans 1:25 NIV). The person requesting this is asking you to violate your conscience.

Sometimes we forget that our conscience is a gift from God, a tool He gave us to point us toward His principles and ways.

> Most of the time, particularly in today's culture, we have developed "false" consciences. These are "programs" in our minds, not our spirits, as to what is right and wrong, and these things (evolution, secularism, humanism, situational ethics, and traditions and doctrines of religious thinking) control what we think is moral and ethical.

> The world's thinking overrides and drowns out the inner voice of the true conscience that God put within us. (For more on this, see http://bibleresources.org/conscience/.)

Fear of a loved one's request can prevent a person from speaking truth. Yet when we speak in truth, we are hiding nothing, nor are we deceiving our loved one whom God created.

Finally, I would have created a stumbling block if I had allowed my father to walk in the false belief that he was someone other than the person God created him to be.

Biblical Truth: *Therefore, I urge you, brothers and sisters, in view of God's mercy, to offer your bodies as a living sacrifice, holy and pleasing to God—this is your true and proper worship. Do not conform to the pattern of this world, but be transformed by the renewing of your mind. Then you will be able to test and approve what God's will is—his good, pleasing and perfect will* (Romans 12:1-2 NIV). *Let us draw near to God with a sincere heart and with the full assurance that faith* *brings, having our hearts sprinkled to cleanse us from a guilty conscience and having our bodies washed with pure water. Let us hold unswervingly to the hope we profess, for he who promised is faithful. And let us consider how we may spur one another on toward love and good deeds* (Hebrews 10:22-24 NIV).

Saying No Does Not Equal Hate.

Our culture tells us that if we do not call our loved one by his or her chosen name and by its accompanying pronouns, we are haters. We do not hate; we simply have convictions and a conscience that we have to live with.

In our culture, if you do not condone and even celebrate such actions, you are seen as the enemy. But if you do give in, you will regret it, and here is the reason: Often the family believes this request will be the end of the matter. But, sadly, it is just the beginning. One boundary crossed sets the stage for the next, and then the next, and so on. I have met parents who did this for their child. They bought into the idea that it was the only thing their child would ask of them. Before long, the daughter or son believed the parents accepted and approved of his or her decision to live as the opposite gender.

You can and should express a great deal of love and sympathy for the struggle your loved one is enduring, but God created your loved one to be male or female. Who are we to say otherwise? We need to keep our eyes on what God calls honest and worthy of our praise. Our personhood, our identity, comes from Him, not from a human surgeon. The fact is, truth breaks bondage.

Biblical Truth: *For you created my inmost being; you knit me together in my mother's womb. I praise you because I am fearfully and wonderfully made; your works are wonderful, I know that full well. My frame was not hidden from you when I was made in the secret place, when I was woven together in the depths of the earth* (Psalm 139:13-15 NIV). *Then you will know the truth, and the truth will set you free* (John 8:32 NIV).

My Gender-Confused Loved One Wants Me to Accept His or Her Cross-Gender Dressing.

In general, most Christians address this type of scenario through Deuteronomy 22:5, which says, *A woman shall not wear a man's garment, nor shall a man put on a woman's cloak, for whoever does these things is an abomination to the LORD your God* (ESV). According to Thayer's lexicon, the Hebrew word for abomination is defined as "a disgusting thing; in the ethical sense, of wickedness." In a sense, cross-dressing is an act of self-deception as well as an attempt to deceive others. It is a misrepresentation: dressing as a woman does not make a man a woman; neither does dressing as a man make a woman a man.

Some will argue that the Deuteronomy passage is in the Old Testament, and therefore it does not pertain to today's world. For example, we do not abide by all the dietary restrictions given in the Mosaic Law. But does that mean we should ignore the Old Testament altogether? Do we really have the freedom to pick and choose what behaviors are acceptable to God?

It is not about your preferences or mine. Accepting or approving of loved ones who are acting outside the parameters of godly conduct only feeds their delusion. It adds power to the compulsiveness of their behavior. If you support their cross-dressing, they are encouraged to travel farther down the path of falsehood. And eventually, they will choose that falsehood, rather than God, as their foundation.

Creating boundaries demonstrates what we are responsible for, and they help us define what we are not responsible for, such as decisions made by our loved one. Creating boundaries helps us distinguish our property lines and helps us take care of ourselves and be good stewards of who we are. God defined who He is when He said to Moses, *"I AM WHO I AM. This is what you are to say to the Israeltites: I AM has sent me to you"* (Exodus 3:14 NIV).

Biblical Truth: *Each one should carry their own load* (Galatians 6:5 NIV). Everyone should carry his or her own responsibilities.

PART 4

Answering Theological Questions

Does God love people who identify as transgender? It would be foolish of me, or anyone, to state that God does not love those who identify as transgender.

First, we each must accept that we live in a fallen world, which resulted from Adam and Eve's sin:

> *Then the eyes of both of them were opened, and they realized they were naked; so they sewed fig leaves together and made coverings for themselves. Then the man and his wife heard the sound of the LORD God as he was walking in the garden in the cool of the day, and they hid from the LORD God among the trees of the garden. But the LORD God called to the man, "Where are you?" He answered, "I heard you in the garden, and I was afraid because I was naked; so I hid." And he said, "Who told you that you were naked? Have you eaten from the tree that I commanded you not to eat from?" The man said, "The woman you put here with me—she gave me some fruit from the tree, and I ate it." Then the LORD God said to the woman, "What is this you have done?" The woman said, "The serpent deceived me, and I ate."* (Genesis 3:7-13 NIV)

Second, Jesus Christ died on the cross to redeem us from the control of sin. *For God so loved the world that he gave his one and only Son, that whoever believes in him shall not perish but have eternal life* (John 3:16 NIV). Jesus Christ died on the cross for humanity. In doing so, He proved His love for each of us by dying for our sins and transgressions. The love of Jesus Christ has been proven for each and every one of us.

Why should members of Christ's church open their hearts to a transgender person? Churches proclaim that they are called to be hospitals for the wounded, yet so often church members turn away the hurting and wounded of the fallen world in which we live. At times, each of us falls into temptations that distance us from God and create havoc in our lives.

We cannot say that when one falls into the temptations of the flesh there is no hope of a redemptive work by the Holy Spirit, *in whom we have redemption, the forgiveness of sins* (Colossians 1:14 NIV). *And all are justified freely by his grace through the redemption that came by Christ Jesus* (Romans 3:24 NIV). May each of us who claim Christianity observe what the Lord says in Jeremiah 2:2—*"I remember the devotion of your youth, how as a bride you loved me"* (NIV).

Let's go back to showing the love of God and recognizing that Christ loves those whom you may find difficult to understand. In spite of their struggle with their identity, they can (and should) find the reflection of Christ's love in us.

Biblical Truth: *Therefore, if anyone is in Christ, the new creation has come: The old has gone, the new is here!* (2 Corinthians 5:17 NIV). Always *be kind and compassionate to one another, forgiving each other, just as in Christ God forgave you* (Ephesians 4:32 NIV).

Does the Bible Specifically Forbid Transgenderism?

The Bible does not use the words *transgender*, *transvestite*, or *trans-anything*. However, it does speak of giving into the lust of the flesh. When a belief or stronghold goes against our Creator, the first seed has been planted. If I say as a female that I am really a male, I am lying. *[By choice] they exchanged the truth of God for a lie, and worshiped and served the creature rather than the Creator, who is blessed forever! Amen* (Romans 1:25 AMP). I would, in a sense, become a victim of this false belief. But speaking in arrogance against the Creator Himself—is that not rebellion? Sure it is.

If I continue to buy into this belief, I will suffer the consequences of that way of thinking: *Therefore God gave them over in the sinful desires of their hearts to sexual impurity for the degrading of their bodies with one another* (Romans 1:24 NIV). My heart would be seeking "self" rather than God. I might think I was correcting what was wrong, but God says, *"Woe to those who call evil good and good evil, who put darkness for light and light for darkness, who put bitter for sweet and sweet for bitter"* (Isaiah 5:20 NIV).

Biblical Truth: God says, *"You will seek me and find me when you seek me with all your heart"* (Jeremiah 29:13 NIV). Each of us must choose.

People Who Identify As Transgender Never Change. Is This True?
Absolutely not! First, if you are a Christian, remember that when you look at the speck of sawdust in your brother's eye, you need to take note of the plank in your own eye (Matthew 7:3). *Who are you to judge someone else's servant? To their own master, servants stand or fall. And they will stand, for the Lord is able to make them stand* (Romans 14:4 NIV).

The Lord looks deep into our messy lives and knows when a person seeks after Him. Too often we write others off and therefore miss the opportunity of investing into lives the Lord desires to redeem. Often He choose to use people such as you or me in the process. (More on this in the next section.)

Biblical Truth: When you look at others, remember, *all have sinned and fall short of the glory of God* (Romans 3:23 NIV).

Is It Possible to Be Transgender and Be a Christian?

This section and the following one are addressed by Kerry Potter, a contributer to the Help 4 Families Newsletter. She said, "Yes, I believe it is, since God's grace comes to us wherever we are when we accept Christ as our Savior."

Is It Possible to Be a Christian and Remain Transgender?

This, says Potter, is an entirely different proposition. For years, I (Potter) found myself in exactly this dilemma, and I found that it is the most miserable of all ways to live. And the reason for that misery was the war going on in my heart, over who was going to control my life.

You see, after years of searching, the Holy Spirit finally brought me to a crucial truth: I could not live for myself (be transgender) and also live for God at the same time. Jesus said, *"Anyone who comes to me but refuses to let go of father, mother, spouse, children, brothers, sisters—yes, even one's own self—can't be my disciple. Anyone who won't shoulder his own cross and follow behind me can't be my disciple"* (Luke 14:26-27 MSG).

I found that to be transgender was to live a self-absorbed life in which my own happiness was paramount over everyone else's. There is no relationship we will not risk, nor any price we will not pay in order to get what we want. All the emotional and physical damage we cause others and ourselves, all the relationships lost or severely broken—to what end? Our personal happiness? Really, is this what God wants for us?

Galatians 5:24 says this: *Those who belong to Christ Jesus have crucified the flesh with its passions and desires* (NIV). Salvation is a gift paid for by Christ's blood, but sanctification (true discipleship) requires the ultimate, total surrender of our lives to the Lord Jesus Christ.

If you try to claim to be a believer in Christ, as I used to do, yet live for yourself, you will live a powerless, defeated life. If you do not believe me, read Romans 7:15-24. But if you will truly surrender everything that you are to our Lord Jesus and allow the Holy Spirit to have His way in your heart, you will find true life, and with it true happiness—that is His promise. Jesus said, *"Whoever wants to save their life will lose it, but whoever loses their life for me will find it"* (Matthew 16:25 NIV).

Walking in Truth: KathyGrace

Even before I went to kindergarten, I knew I wanted to be a boy; I should have been a boy. I would ride my tricycle over to my girlfriend's house to pick her up so we could get married. But I also knew that how I felt had to be a secret. Otherwise, I would be rejected and probably punished by my dad.

My home life was awful. Neither my mom nor my dad had the emotional tools to relate to me, or to my siblings for that matter. My dad was emotionally and verbally abusive to my mom, constantly accusing her of things that were not true. This led me to the conclusion that women are hated; men see nothing good about women. I also watched my mom crumble under the weight of my dad's words and treatment, and I learned that women were weak and vulnerable. It is not safe to be a woman; men have all the control. I was certain all those things were true, so why would I want to be a woman?

Starting school was awful. I had to be someone I did not like, and I could not be who I felt I was. I liked being a tough tomboy, detached from my emotions. I felt I was not important to anyone, so if I did not feel anything, my heart would be protected, and I could not be hurt. This also kept people from getting too close. I did have friends, but I did not want a best friend. Being liked was too risky, and so was sharing secrets. If my secret desire to become a man was rejected, then I would be rejected.

Two years after starting school, my little brother was born. He was cherished and adored. The shaky relationship I had with my dad disappeared; I was totally replaced by this baby boy. I began to believe that not only are women hated, weak, and vulnerable, they can also be discarded and replaced. It proved once again it was not safe to be a woman. To be noticed and have value, you have to be a man. A few years later, my older brother molested me, which confirmed my beliefs that women are weak, vulnerable, and hated, and it is not safe to be a woman. Men have all the control and have more value.

One summer, I finally made a friend. As I grew to trust this neighbor boy, I finally decided to share my secret of wanting to be a man. His response was "Cool, now we can be brothers." This affirmation made me feel that becoming a man was the right decision. Going into high school, I began to research how I could make this happen. Meanwhile, the neighbor boy and I went roller skating and picked up girls. I got a car at sixteen and started living a double life. At school and home I was a girl; out with my friend, I was a boy.

Through my research, I found a doctor who would help me, and at nineteen, I moved out of the house and in with a family to begin to live as a man. This was the most exhilarating time for me. I changed my name and began to live as Keith. I felt so free, so alive. Nothing stood in the way of my happiness any longer. The two daughters of the family were excited to have me live with their family because they did not have an older brother. They invited me to go to the church youth group with them. I finally gave in and went. After about a month of going, I accepted Jesus as my Lord and Savior.

I was not sure what Jesus thought about me, but because He did not strike me down with lightning, I believed He was okay with my choice. I had been involved with the church for about a year when I was approached by the pastor there. He called me into his office and said he had heard a rumor about me. He asked me who I was, really. I told him I was a man who used to be a woman. He said, "We love you, but don't come back here." So I left the church, but not the Lord.

After two failed relationships with nice girls, I got more involved in church. I made room for the Lord everywhere in my life. I got involved in music ministry, youth work, and leading a Bible study. I was incredibly hungry for the Lord. At the same time, I had become addicted to pornography. I was ashamed of it, but the addiction was great, and there did not seem to be anywhere I could go for help.

One night, on my way to orchestra practice, I heard the Lord's voice asking me, "Will you now? Will you now?" I took an inventory of my life and found I had nothing to lose, so I said, "Yes, Lord, I will." I had no idea what I was saying yes to, but I knew I wanted it. Nothing seemed different that night, but three months later, I realized my addiction to pornography was gone. Saying yes to the Lord had delivered me from pornography—forever.

Over the next four years, the Lord drew me to Himself. He provided spiritual parents to begin my healing and to show me what family really is. The Lord showed me He was very interested in me and really wanted me to know He loved me. It was scary at first to have the big, omnipotent God chasing me, but it also attracted me. Most of the time, I was so overwhelmed by Him, and so desperate at the same time, that I thought I was going to explode. Then one night, after a Sunday evening service, my spiritual father wanted to talk to me.

I knew something was up, and it felt like I was about to be confronted—again. We went back into a prayer room, and there sat a pastor waiting for us. I thought, Yep, here we go. I sat down and the pastor said to me, "I'm hearing some rumors about you, and I'm wondering, who are you? Who are you, really?" The same question as before, but this time I told the truth. Instead of saying, "I am a man who used to be a woman," I said, "I am a woman living as a man."

Right after I spoke that, the Holy Spirit blew into me, and I realized that to really know Jesus I had to go back to being a woman. If I wanted the relationship I had been seeking, there was no other choice than to walk in the truth. I saw the next two weeks of my life and all I had to do. I saw the ministries I had to step down from, the people I needed to talk to. I knew I needed to break up with my girlfriend that night. There was no other choice.

At first, the pastor had no advice to offer. When I told the pastor what I had seen and what I thought I should do, he said he thought that was the correct thing too and that he would walk with me through the process. I started as soon as I left the room. I found my girlfriend, and after explaining who I really was, I broke up with her. The next day I was fired, but I knew this was the Lord clearing the path for me.

The next two weeks were filled with the things God had shown me—meeting with pastors, stepping down from ministry positions, and telling the truth about why I was doing it. I am sure I blew a few of their minds. The Lord made it clear I needed to leave that church in order to leave old thought patterns behind, and my pastor agreed. So I moved from Vancouver back to Oregon to start all over.

I also met with the women's ministry leader of the Portland Fellowship. I had heard of them through some of the circumstances surrounding my new life. I was eager to call and get on with it. We first met in March, but the next program did not start until September. Oh, that seemed so long to wait!

The first year of transitioning was hard. I was so depressed and had so much to learn, but God provided so much grace. At the time, I did not realize how overwhelmingly heavy the depression was. It took all morning to take a shower and get ready for the day. I asked the Lord every day, "Who do You say that I am? What do You say?" I thought He needed to change my hair, my voice, and make me feminine—now.

But after three straight days of telling Him that, He said those things did not matter. What? He did not care about that? He said to me, "I don't care about those things; I'm after your heart." All I could say then was "Oh." And after my heart He was. The godly woman he brought to mentor me spoke the truth and kept me in the Word. She put up with a lot from me in my immaturity and lack of understanding.

The Lord began to walk me through the dad stuff. One day, during my prayer time, the Lord said, "When you pray, I want you to call Me Daddy." I said very loudly, "I'm *not* doing that!" My father had made

Daddy seem like a swear word to me, and now the Lord wanted me to call Him that. No way. Not now, not ever. But the Lord persisted. Finally, I thought, what is this really going to hurt? So, quietly, I spoke it. "Daddy?"

Something inside broke. I began to cry, and then an anger rose up in me and I began to pound on the ground yelling, "I hate you. I hate you. I hate you!" Then the Lord wrapped His love around me like a blanket, and He held me close. As I sat there recovering, something was different. I told the Lord I really did not hate Him. He said, "I know, but you had to for a moment. I can take it." The next day something was out of the way between me and the Lord. My view of Him was different. A new place in my heart was open to Him, and though He had not moved, I had. I had moved closer.

After that first year, I finally got a job, but because the physical changes were not complete, I got a job as Keith. I worked there as a man for three years, but as I continued figuring out who I was as a woman at night, being called Keith was uncomfortable. I realized I was leading a double life, as I had lived in high school. Something needed to change.

Although I was discouraged in my first attempt at finding a new job, I told the Lord I was quitting my job at the end of the month and He better figure something out. I went to work the next day and gave my notice. Two weeks later, the Lord told me to try the same place again, and this time there was an opening. I started that job the day after the other one ended. It was my first job working as a woman.

The Lord made this a safe and supportive place for me as I

continued learning to live as a woman. Even the kind of work I was doing affirmed my identity as a woman. I was a baker. One night, as I was thanking the Lord for my job, I began to laugh because I was a baker and, after all, that was women's work, right? The Lord said, "You are who you were created to be; now walk in that."

During those transitional four years, I was also attending the Portland Fellowship (PF) program. It was a very safe place for me to just "be" as I figured out all this stuff. They did not tell me how I had to act or dress. Instead, they walked beside me with encouragement and helped me discover the truth—the truth about the Lord and who I am. They rejoiced with me in my victories and picked me up when I fell. They facilitated the healing and freedom I now walk in. The Lord used them mightily in my life.

During my fifth year at PF, I became a small-group leader. I wanted to pour into others what had been poured into me. I wanted to hold out hope, as it had been held out to me. But that year was hard. It was hard to watch people give up on God and go back into the lifestyle. And after a few years of being a small-group leader, I realized my testimony was preventing people from getting to know the woman I had become. So I decided to step away from PF for a season so I could figure out who I was, just me, without anyone knowing anything about me.

I started attending a church and found a women's Bible study to go to. Although I thought I had quite a few things figured out, I felt both stretched and lost in this women's world. But the Lord knew what I needed and brought around me the women necessary to continue the growth process.

Eventually, I opened up to them and shared my experiences, which brought an even greater healing and friendship. I began to see my struggle to figure out how to be a woman was normal. As I realized the other women were asking the same questions I was, I saw that my quest to becoming all that God created me to be was their quest too. We were all in this together!

When I was ready to return to PF, I started back on the prayer team. After that, the Lord graciously made it very clear that He wanted me to become a small-group leader again. And in order to answer even more of my questions, the Lord arranged for me to teach on femininity. I thought, Huh, me? You want me to teach? What do I have to offer? But I accepted.

On the way home, I asked the Lord, "What have you gotten me into now? You know that since I am signed up to do this, You are now signed up too." As I continued to ponder this, a realization hit me, and I began to laugh. What a slap in the enemy's face for me to teach on femininity! I think I heard the Lord chuckle too. I have continued to teach and lead small groups. Each year I am changed by seeing the Lord meet each person and the transformation I witness in the hearts of those who come.

In 2015, I celebrated twenty-two years of walking out of the lifestyle and into the truth. Although it was hard, I would do it all over again because of the fruit, healing, and freedom that is now mine. I also know I would not have made it this far without Jesus as my Lord and Savior. Without His grace and mercy surrounding my life, I would still be in that life, not knowing there is a better way. He arranged the support and fellowship I needed all along the way.

We are not meant to walk alone or carry a struggle by ourselves. This is my testimony of the love story between our Savior and His beloved.

Benjamin's Story

Over the past twenty years, I have been wrestling with my gender identity and my feelings of disgust with being a male and desiring to be female. Yet, through that, I have come to learn and see more about this condition and the circumstances that have shaped this issue within me. I have seen God's faithfulness and His love. Through this, I have seen how God has led me to a place that is of His purpose, and I have embraced the idea of dying to self and living to Christ. This is my story and the way in which this has been developing within me. I hope that through this story someone might be helped.

I was born into a Christian family. My parents are both followers of Jesus Christ, and they discipled me and my siblings to follow Him as well. I am the oldest of three boys. My father was a pastor off and on and led several churches. I saw both the good and the bad side of church politics, which has had a deep impact on me in several areas, including my gender and my battle with transsexuality.

I put my faith in Jesus at the age of five, and my adoption into His family and the presence of the Holy Spirit in my life has provided a tether that has tied me to God and protected me through the decades as I have worked through my gender-identity issues. God is faithful.

When I was five, my dad was the pastor of a small Baptist church in central Texas. Because of my parents' decision to homeschool, this church decided to force us to leave. That was my first taste of what a church that is not putting Christ first can do to its pastor and his family.

After this, my parents were very disillusioned, and eventually our family moved to Washington State, as there was not much going for us in central Texas.

After a couple years in Washington, God again impressed upon my dad the calling to pursue full-time ministry at a church, and he eventually accepted the role of pastor at a small church. He served there for a couple years, and we made several good relationships. Yet there were also some influential families in the church that did not approve of my dad's style and did not accept him. They eventually worked to drive him out.

One night a letter was circulated among the church families that was hateful toward my dad. My mom came into my bedroom, told me what happened, and said that we needed to pray for my dad. That night, I asked my mom, "Why do people hate my dad so much?"

The church eventually voted him out, and I watched my father melt. It seemed to me that he mentally and emotionally collapsed. He spent hours in the garage whittling a large stick.

As a boy of about ten or eleven years of age, I watched my father get hurt by church people. Since I was the oldest of the children, my mom began to lean on me in ways I was not equipped or able to handle. It was too much for me to deal with on my own. Because of that trauma, I sought an escape.

At first, I fantasized about being a cartoon character, and I imagined what it would be like to change myself into that character and

54

live like him. Then that morphed into imagining myself as a cat. I drew diagrams of how I could surgically be transformed into a cat, and I fantasized about it.

Growing up, I could look back and see tendencies that I could easily interpret as things that drew me in and supported my longing to be the opposite gender. I have often been drawn to female friends and relationships. I very much resonated with things that were stereotypically female more than things that were considered male. Growing up, my closest friends were, more often than not, girls. At times, people made fun of my friendships, but it always felt more natural or comfortable.

I was introduced to the idea of transitioning from male to female through a daytime TV talk show. My mom often had a talk show running. One day, the show's theme revolved around inviting guests on stage and having them talk about a childhood friend they had not seen in years.

After the brief dialogue with the guests recalling stories from their past, the host then welcomed the long-lost friend onstage and the guests could see how much had changed. One guest talked about a boy he was close to growing up and how the two of them played basketball together. The host then welcomed the friend, and onto the stage walked a woman. She was one of the most beautiful women I had ever seen. The host and audience began talking and asking questions about how this person transitioned from a boy playing basketball to a tall, slender, beautiful woman.

At that point, I realized my desire to be someone else was entirely possible. I became obsessed with the concept of transitioning from a boy to a girl. It would be a dream come true. From then on, I felt I knew that was what I was supposed to be. I was a girl, and I needed my body to show it. I often planned and fantasized about how and when I could make the transition.

I knew it was not something I could talk to my parents about. I knew my parents would not approve or support it, and, because of that disapproval, I knew God would not approve either (although I was not really able to state why).

In several ways, I had a very judgmental and condemning view of God and therefore guilt, shame, and fear helped to keep me from pursuing this more than I did. As often as I could, I actively engaged in feeding my craving and fantasy, but I did so secretly and privately. I became very good at covering my tracks.

I started to dress up in my mom's clothes. My mom is a very short woman, and by the time I was twelve, we were about the same height. I often sneaked into my parent's closet while the family was away or in another area of the house and dressed up in my mom's clothes. I wore her makeup and stood in front of the mirror and longed to be that person I saw. I then took great care to clean everything up and put everything back the way I found it, hoping that no one would find anything out of place or suspect anyone had been there. As far as I know, no one ever knew.

I looked ahead to getting out on my own and entering college. Once I got out of the house, I could pursue my dream. I could not wait. At times, I prayed that God would make me a girl. I begged Him to let me go to sleep and wake up the next morning as a girl, and everything would be the way I felt it should have been all along. Needless to say, that did not happen.

On the flipside, I also begged God over and over to please take the struggle and the feelings away. There were times I cried and writhed about it. I longed so much to change my gender and be a girl, but I knew it was not right, and I begged God to take the desire away.

I also pleaded with God to tell me why I had to deal with it. It became a daily thing. I cannot remember a single day in which my desire to be the opposite gender has not played a role. I prayed and struggled, but the feelings and desires were still there.

I probably also knew that, because of my guilt, fear, and loyalty to my family, I would not actually pursue the dream. I could not bear the thought of the hurt and pain I would bring to them if I did pursue a gender change. The thought that I might not be welcome to see them again was something I could not face.

Within my family, this subject was never really discussed. My parents eventually found out one day and made it very clear that they were opposed to it. That just reinforced my feelings that if I ever did pursue a gender change, I very likely would not see my family much again. At the same time, in my family there was a pervading thought that if you just ignored something and did not feed it with your thoughts, it would eventually die. That may have been their plan to deal with their son's gender identity crisis: If we do not talk about it, it will die. But not dealing with it was simply that, not dealing with it, and it did not go away.

Eventually, I went to college. That was supposed to be the point at which I would live the life I wanted, be the person I wanted to be, and transition into a female. Plagued with guilt and knowing it would destroy my parents, I could not do it. It was disappointing in the most severe sense of the word.

I knew I would not pursue this lifestyle, although everything in me wanted it. As much as I wanted to, as much as I played around in secret with cross-dressing and engaging with transsexuals online, I could not go through with anything beyond that. I was cross-dressing regularly in secret. I purchased some clothes, dressed up, felt guilty, and then discarded the clothes. It was a cycle. I bought menopause pills from the store because I had read they contained small doses of hormones. I took one dose and began to feel very guilty. I flushed the remainder of the pills down the toilet in my college dorm.

Perhaps the biggest issue for me during this journey has been the loneliness. I felt that this issue is not one that Christians, who should be the ones I can turn to, know how to deal with—as though it is a great taboo issue that extra-special dirty people wrestle with—and it made me feel very much alone. My general experience with sharing my story or struggle with a few pastors—hoping for some discipleship and help—has been some good-hearted intentions to pray with me. But they were utterly unprepared for what to do to help me, so the issue never came up again.

Again, through these experiences, the idea pressed harder and harder into my mind that I was alone in this struggle. There are those who wrestle with it and apparently find relief in pursuing a change of gender through therapy, hormones, and engaging as the opposite gender. I looked up information online for "Christian transgender" or "Transgender ministry" or something like that. The results were discouraging in many ways. I found several sites that were touted as Christian and that condoned transsexuality. They supported the idea that one can be a good Christian man who goes through the proper treatments and becomes a good Christian woman. I could not find anything that was for those who had a strong conviction that what they were so strongly drawn to was not right. Even though I had trouble at the time putting my finger on why, I knew transsexuality was not something God wanted me to pursue.

I went to a college men's group for a while, looking for some accountability and help, but no one there was able to deal with it. The group was focused on staying pure (resisting pornography and masturbation). I did not connect with them; my problems were not quite the same.

Shortly after college, I got married. My relationship with my parents was becoming more distant, so as a husband I had someone else to fight for. In some ways, I really hoped that being married would help to take away the longing to change my gender. My hope was that it would ease the battle and make the struggle less intense. But it did not help. It did not take the desires away, but God has used my marriage to improve me. I believe that if it was not for my wife, I would be living a life immersed in my gender confusion and struggling to find value and worth. God is faithful!

After we had been married a short time, I realized that I needed additional help and that I was desperately struggling. By the grace of God, I came across the first resource I had ever seen that dealt specifically with gender identity from a biblical perspective. It was a huge step for me to contact the leader, Jerry. He was very gracious to visit with me. For about a year or so, I met with him over the phone, once every other week or so.

It was through these conversations that my view of this issue radically changed. Jerry was very up-front with me that he was not a clinical counselor but someone who understands this struggle and had walked it longer and farther than I had. He truly helped me to dig into the reasoning behind the struggle. We explored the "why." I started to see how the trauma and pain I experienced growing up led me to seek an escape.

As a young boy, the retreat to the feminine was that escape. Jesus said in John 8:32, *"You will know the truth, and the truth will set you free"* (NIV). As much as I want to believe that I am a woman in a man's body, there is nothing but my imagination telling me that. It is just not true. I desire to live in the truth.

Over the years, I have realized that, no matter how hard it might be to find at times, I need to pursue community with others. I have taken part in Celebrate Recovery and Help 4 Families, which have been God-sends for me. God is so faithful! He never gave up on me, and He is now using the relationships I have with others who are walking through similar journeys as together we struggle with transgender issues. God is restoring us.

He is also allowing me to use my story to help others. It has been an incredible journey to see how God can take something that is sinful and isolating, then restore me and use that struggle to let others know they are not alone. I have been there too, and I know God is always desiring them to know and rest in Him.

God is so faithful. Through continued accountability and being surrounded by a loving wife and community, God has been faithful to keep me focused on what is important.

The feelings are not gone, and the desire is still there, but, unlike before, I am not walking this path alone, and my God is stronger still.

PART 5

Christianity and Culture

Our culture believes some people are born transgender. How did this belief arise? Possibly, this fallacy came from people who struggled and prayed for years for God to release them from their unusual desires. When they did not experience the release they prayed for, they very likely concluded that God was implicitly telling them He approved of their desires to be the opposite gender.

The enemy has whispered lies into the hearts of those who think God made a mistake in creating them. Our confused culture has largely endorsed those lies and, in the process, led many into a form of slavery. Paul compares our sinful nature, our flesh, to a slave (see Romans 6:15-23). Slaves must obey their masters, and our sinful nature naturally obeys our fleshly desires. That is especially true for one who has grown weary of the internal battle. While cultures change and frequently revise morality codes, the Bible never changes; it stands firm because it is based on God's immutable, holy character.

Biblical Truth: *Jesus Christ is the same yesterday and today and forever* (Hebrews 13:8 NIV).

How Do I Explain to People That Christianity Is Not about Hate, but about the Truth of God?

Those who do not know God do not know His love. Some do not understand how a God of love can allow any pain in the world, let alone mind-controlling issues such as transgenderism. Again, it is crucial to remember that we live in a fallen world. Sin is real, and it is pervasive. Yet the Scriptures are very clear that the God who is love also judges sin: *And the heavens proclaim his righteousness, for he is a God of justice* (Psalm 50:6 NIV). Often, those who accept false views of God—and that includes denying His holiness—do so because they refuse to accept His boundaries.

God is not a killjoy whose great desire is to spoil our fun. He knows, far better than we do, what is good for us and what will harm us, so He set boundaries to keep us from harming ourselves. The principle here is the same as a parent of a toddler placing a gate in front of the stairs to prevent the child from a tragic accident. The toddler may not like the gate, but it is there for his protection. Christians who warn others of the dangers of crossing God's boundaries are expressing God's protective love.

Biblical Truth: *For the LORD is our judge, the LORD is our lawgiver, the LORD is our king; it is he who will save us* (Isaiah 33:22 NIV).

Our Loved One Has Embraced the Belief That People Are Born Transgender. How Do We Tell Him or Her Otherwise?
Very likely, this false perception came after a person spent years praying for God to remove the desires. Paul knew of struggles with the flesh (Romans 7 chronicles his war within). He wrote, *For I have the*

desire to do what is good, but I cannot carry it out. For I do not do the good I want to do, but the evil I do not want to do—this I keep on doing. Now if I do what I do not want to do, it is no longer I who do it, but it is sin living in me that does it (Romans 7:18-20 NIV).

Such an internal battle can seem especially difficult to accept regarding children, and specifically regarding children who struggle with gender dysphoria. It seems unjust to us that a loving God would allow a child to suffer in this way. I understand this view, but if we allow our thoughts to take this form we are forgetting that we live in a fallen world where others impact children by their actions and their relationships.

Very often children who suffer with this dysphoria have heard many lies about gender issues, and those lies have taken root. If the child repeatedly succumbs to those lies, eventually he or she will become enslaved.

This is especially true when one has grown weary of the battle raging inside the heart and mind. Satan tries to steal a person's true identity because it offers not only freedom but also a recognition of who one truly is and who their Creator is. Our sinful nature obeys its fleshly desires if we give in to those desires. Only the unchanging Bible shows us the truly sinful condition of our heart and gives us the cure for such a condition.

Biblical Truth: *For the flesh desires what is contrary to the Spirit, and the Spirit what is contrary to the flesh. They are in conflict with* *each other so that you are not to do whatever you want* (Galatians 5:17 NIV). *There is one who speaks rashly like the thrusts of a sword, but the tongue of the wise brings healing* (Proverbs 12:18 NASB).

Why Should the Church Open Their Hearts to Transgender People?

Are transgenders really all that different from anyone else? We are all sinners; we all have struggles of the flesh at some level. The church can bring true hope to those who identify as transgender. If we abandon these lost ones to the culture, they will hear only the wrong message: they will hear that their lifestyle is acceptable and to be celebrated.

No one will tell them they can escape their destructive ways. No one will explain to them the need to repent. And, as Proverbs 28:13 says, *Whoever conceals their sins does not prosper, but the one who confesses and renounces them finds mercy* (NIV). Churches—Christians—are obliged to carry the truth to the lost and hurting, and the lost and hurting include transgenders. Jesus said, *"I have not come to call the righteous, but sinners"* (Mark 2:17 NIV). If we claim to follow Him, we are to do the same—to call sinners to Jesus.

Biblical Truth: God has entrusted to churches the responsibility of loving the lost so they will see that *there is a way that appears to be right, but in the end it leads to [the] death [of who God created them to be]* (Proverbs 14:12 NIV).

PART 6

Moving Forward with God!

Memories

When your loved one asks you to approve of his or her choice to change gender, your heart aches. In essence, that person is asking you to erase years of memories, to reject the person you know and to love and accept a replacement. This reminds me of what Nehemiah faced when he returned to Jerusalem after the Israelites' seventy-year-long captivity in Babylon:

> [He] must have had flashbacks—mental pictures of the life of his Jewish ancestors, a life that no longer existed. All he could see now was the burned rubble, evidence of the enemy invasion that destroyed homes, left families divided, and removed the brightest and most-talented among them as hostages. How his heart must have ached! Like Nehemiah, we are flooded with memories of what used to be. (Wagstaff, p. 42)

When I received my first letter from my dad with the name "Becky" on the return address, I held it in my hands and stared at it. My heart ached; my dad had been taken into captivity. Just like Nehemiah, we experience losses:

> Discovering that a family member is transgender can be particularly devastating, especially when that person cuts himself or herself off from the family. When this occurs, the family may feel almost as if that person had died. And in truth, many of our dreams and expectations for that loved one may die. (Wagstaff, p. 42)

66

We long for the days before a loved one's transsexuality changed everything. We wish the problem would go away. We want the situation we are facing to disappear. We long for an end to the conflicts among family members, the unending questions, the guilt trips, the deception, and, most of all, the pain it has brought. We want everything to go back to the way it was.

However, sometimes we are unaware that God wants to do to a work in our lives, a work that will draw us closer to Him and glorify Him. He wants to bring us to new growth and maturity that otherwise may not have happened. No doubt about it, having a close relationship with God the Father and His Son, Jesus Christ, will bring us comfort and peace that no one else and nothing else can offer.

Biblical Truth: *The mind governed by the flesh is death, but the mind governed by the Spirit is life and peace* (Romans 8:6 NIV). God longs to *rebuild the ancient ruins and restore the places long devastated* (Isaiah 61:4 NIV).

Recognize Your Hurt. Everyone has hurts; everyone carries pain and burdens. What may hurt most is knowing you love Christ, yet you do not understand why you are facing this situation. You are told to release your faith, claim a promise, confess a cure, and walk away from your despair.

That is all well and good, but this kind of preaching may come from Christians who have not experienced much suffering. They are like Job's babysitters; they knew all the answers, but they could not relieve his pain. Job said to them, *ye are all physicians of no value* (Job 13:4 KJV).

> Thank God for well-meaning friends, but if they could experience your agony for even one hour, they would think differently. Put them in your place just once, feeling what you feel, experiencing the inner pain you carry, and they would say to you, "How in the world can you take it? I couldn't handle what you are going through!" (Wilkerson, p.16).

How true this is.

We want others to understand; however, although they can be sympathetic, unless they walk this journey and we walk theirs, no one can truly understand what and how you feel. But, through prayer, we have someone who does understand our pain. We cannot carry our cross alone. Jesus knows this.

> The truth is, Jesus was too weak and frail to carry His cross. It was laid on another's shoulders. He reached the end of His endurance. He was a physically broken and wounded man.
> There is only so much a person can take. There is a breaking point. (Wilkerson, p. 22)

This is the reason Simon Cryrene came to Jesus to help lift the weight of the burden laid upon Him.

When we are wrung out and have nothing left, we come to understand His strength is made perfect in our weakness. Through His strength we can live to see tomorrow. Paul wrote, *And [the Lord] said unto me, "My grace is sufficient for thee: for my strength is made perfect in weaknes"…. Most gladly therefore will I rather glory in my infirmities, that the power of Christ may rest upon me .... For when I am weak, then am I strong* (2 Corinthians 12:9-10 KJV).

When you feel you are unable to carry on, rest in knowing that God will give you the strength to take each day for what it is. He will not leave you; He will lead you each step of the way. This means you can *trust in the LORD with all your heart and lean not on your own understanding* (Proverbs 3:5 NIV). Is this always going to be easy? No, but it will be possible as you draw nearer to Him and rest in the assurance that comes only from Christ. Sometimes we are tempted to call a friend to help when our real need is to pray, to cry out to Him. Nothing else will fill us like His Holy Spirit's presence.

This journey calls for us to look to Him, and *in all your ways submit to him, and he will make your paths straight* (Proverbs 3:6 NIV).

Once you take this step, you are on your way to facing circumstances with assurance that you will be okay. Speaking of Jesus, Ephesians 3:12 says, *"In him and through faith in him we may approach God with freedom and confidence* (NIV). May you be *confident of this, that he who began a good work in you will carry it on to completion until the day of Christ Jesus* (Philippians 1:6). You will make it. After all, you belong to Him!

Importance of Boundaries

Boundaries are an unavoidable part of our everyday lives. Some boundaries are clearly marked: KEEP OFF THE GRASS, NO TRESPASSING or. FACULTY AREA ONLY. Other boundaries might not be as obvious—at least initially. Perhaps no governmental agency put up a fence or a warning sign, but as you approach the edge of a dangerous precipice, the boundary becomes obvious. That is a boundary you would cross only once. If you cross it, you will die.

Similarly, God fenced off portions of His creation as a protective measure. To the first people He created, God said, *"You are free to eat from any tree in the garden; but you must not eat from the tree of the knowledge of good and evil, for when you eat from it you will certainly die"* (Genesis 2:16-17).

God even surrounds Himself with boundaries:

And the LORD said to Moses, "Go to the people and consecrate them today and tomorrow. Have them wash their clothes and be ready by the third day, because on that day the LORD will come down on Mount Sinai in the sight of all the people. Put limits for the people around the mountain and tell them, 'Be careful that you do not approach the mountain or touch the foot of it. Whoever touches the mountain is to be put to death. They are to be stoned or shot with arrows; not a hand is to be laid on them. No person or animal shall be permitted to live.' Only when the ram's horn sounds a long blast may they approach the mountain." (Exodus 19:10-13 NIV)

After God gave Moses the warning about the people's approach at Mount Sinai, He gave them many laws—not to harm them, but to help them to live in harmony together. Smack dab in the middle of those many specific laws, God gave this one, part of which is quoted repeatedly in the New Testament: The LORD said, *"Do not hate a fellow Israelite in your heart.* Rebuke your neighbor frankly so you will

70

not share in their guilt. *Do not seek revenge or bear a grudge against anyone among your people,* but love your neighbor as yourself. *I am the LORD"* (Leviticus 19:17-18, emphasis added).

Each of the many laws God gave was some sort of boundary, all aimed at loving one's neighbor as oneself. But part of being a good neighbor is rebuking our neighbor (helping him to see he has crossed the boundary line) when we see him going astray. Failure to do so is a failure to really love him—and it places the neighbor who neglects necessary rebukes in a position to share in the wayward neighbor's guilt.

Boundaries define us. In a sense, they send out a message about who we are and who we are not—of what kind of neighbor we are. They define what we are and are not responsible for.

God could not make choices for people to whom He had given free will, so He had to set boundaries for them—for their own good and to preserve His character. I learned that I could not make choices for my father. All I could do was set boundaries—for my dad's good and to preserve my family's character.

Boundaries are not bad things; they are meant to protect us and our loved ones. Each of us must choose whether or not we will create healthy boundaries.

Biblical Truth: *LORD, you alone are my portion and my cup; you make my lot secure. The boundary lines have fallen for me in pleasant places; surely I have a delightful inheritance* (Psalm 16:5-6 NIV). What a boundary blessing upon God's people!

How Should We Pray for Our Lost Loved Ones?

Having a loved one who engages in ungodly gender or sexual behaviors is difficult and heart-wrenching. Family members are not able to mend the sexual and relational brokenness the confused loved one has experienced. But God can do what family members cannot do.

Although our lives may be filled with pain, we must remember we are not powerless. God has given us a remarkable tool to fight on behalf of our confused loved ones. Prayer is our weapon, and no one can take it from us.

God has incomprehensible power, and you can be active on your loved one's behalf by becoming a prayer warrior.

The starting point is to remember the price Jesus paid for all our sins, including those of your confused loved one. When Jesus died upon the cross, the price was paid—fully. This truth can give us confidence when approaching our loving God on behalf of our loved ones.

Your loved ones belong to God, and it is time go to battle for them. Do not lose heart. Pray with persistence. When you rise in the morning, or before you lay your head down in the evening, find a peaceful place where you can have your quiet time with the Lord. Remember that Jesus encourages His followers to *pray and not give up* (Luke 18:1 NIV).

Ask God to give your loved one a thirst to come to Jesus and know Him, for He is filled with the love your loved one needs. Ask God to stir your loved one and give him or her a hunger to search for truth. Ask God to bring a loving, witnessing Christian to your loved one.

Finally, remember this: If you do not pray for your loved one, who will? No other person loves him or her as you do, so no one else can pray with the heartfelt conviction you have.

Biblical Truth: *Do not be anxious about anything, but in everything by prayer and supplication with thanksgiving let your requests be made known to God. And the peace of God, which surpasses all understanding, will guard your hearts and your minds in Christ Jesus* (Philippians 4:6-7 ESV).

Prayer Offered on Your Loved One's Behalf

Dear God, You brought _____ (your loved one's name) into existence for Your glory. I stand in the gap for my loved one, and I proclaim that the devil cannot have him (or her). I ask that my loved one be unable to escape You and the love You have for him (or her) so they he (or she) will reconsider his (or her) life and the decisions he (or she) has made.

May my loved one understand the sin in his (or her) life and repent from it. Show him (or her) what he (or she) is doing wrong. I ask for a release of the ungodly ways and the bad influences in my loved one's life.

I ask for my loved one to develop a godly heart. May God be glorified in and through my loved one. In the name of Jesus Christ, I ask that my loved one come to serve You. Loosen the chains of bondage; open his (or her) eyes from the darkness, and set my loved one free. Amen.

Compassion Is at the Heart of the Gospel

Because of God's compassion, He sent His Son to save a world full of sinners. Without doubt, the world is a better place when human hearts, like God's heart, are moved by compassion. But compassion does not—cannot—stand alone. In this fallen world, sin has consequences. So while we must treat our fellow sinners with godly compassion, we also must treat sin with godly disdain. God's Word simply does not allow for using compassion as an excuse for sin. As Jesus said to the woman caught in adultery (along with a sinning man), *"Then neither do I condemn you. ... Go now and leave your life of sin"* (John 8:11 NIV).

Jesus' command to "leave your life of sin," harsh as it might sound, also flows from His compassion. He knew that if the woman continued in her lifestyle, her sins would continue to damage her and hinder her ability to live a rich, full life. What's more, her sins would have harmed others.

When we use that inborn tendency to sin—in whatever form, including effeminacy, as referred to in 1 Corinthians 6:9—as an excuse to continue committing the same sin, then we hurt ourselves and those around us.

Yes, Christians must treat gender dysphoric people with compassion, but excusing and enabling their behavior will help no one. True compassion says not only "Neither do I condemn you," but also

"Go and leave your life of sin."

In Conclusion, Help 4 Families believes God created distinct genders and at conception assigns a gender to each person. *Then the LORD God made a woman from the rib he had taken out of the man, and he brought her to the man* (Genesis 2:22 NIV). A person's gender is an immutable biological reality and a reminder of God's creation of male and female.

Often the culture looks for a quick fix instead of looking to God for the deep, internal healing needed by one with gender stress. Hormones and surgery only change the appearance of one's outward features, while ignoring the person's heart and soul issues that need appropriate, loving attention.

We encourage families and pastors to discern God's ways—His heart—when seeking to help a loved one through the difficult journey of gender brokenness. May you offer compassionate mentorship and care for the loved ones who reject the God-given gift of their natural gender.

Readings:

A Mother's Devotional. Lillypad/Help 4 Families

A Wife's Perspective. Help 4 Families/Denise Shick

Bold Love. Dr. Dan B. Allender & Dr. Tremper Longman III

Boundaries. Dr. Henry Cloud & Dr. John Townsend

Dangerous Affirmations. Help 4 Families/Denise Shick

Grieving with Hope: Finding Comfort As You Journey through Loss.
    Samuel J. Hodges IV & Kathy Leonard

How to Forgive When You Don't Feel Like It. June Hunt

How to Deal with Difficult Relationships. June Hunt

My Daddy's Secret. Denise Shick & Jerry Gramckow

Reconcilation (DVD). Chad Ahrendt

Seeing Yourself Through God's Eyes. (31-Day Devotional). June Hunt

Understanding Gender Confusion:A Faith-Based Perspective. Denise
    Shick

When Hope Seems Lost. Denise Shick & Help 4 Families

You'll Get Through This. Max Lucado

References:

Cloud, H., Dr., & Townsend, J., Dr. (1992) *Boundaries*. Grand Rapids, MI: Zondervan.

Dillworth, Marc S. (pg. 6-20) www.help4families.com

Fitzgibbons, Rick, M.D., January 12, 2015. "Gender Identity Disorder in Children: Will Jack Be Happier If We All Pretend He's Jill" Aleteia, January 12, 2015, accessed August 24, 2015

Israel, G. E., & D. E. Tarver (1997) *Transgender Care*. Philadelphia, PA: Temple University Press.

McHugh, (2011) Controversial Therapy for Pre-Teen Transgender Patient Raises Questions, accessed August 24, 2015. http://www.foxnews.com/us/2011/10/17/controversial-therapy-for-young-transgender-patients-raises-questions/

Moberly E. (1983) *Homosexuality: A New Christian Ethic*. Cambridge, England: James Clarke & Co.

Savic, I. and Arver, S. (2011) Sex Dimorphism of the Brain in Male-to-Female Transsexuals. *Cerebral Cortex*

Zhou, Y., Lin, F.C., Du, Y.S., Qin, L.D., Zhao, Z.M., Xu, J.R. and Lei, H. (2009) "Gray Matter Abnormalities in Internet Addiction: A Voxel-based Morphometry Study." *European Journal of Radiology*.

Wagstaff, Carol. (2010) *The Lord Comforts*. Living Stones Ministry

Whitehead, N., & Hutt, L. (2011, April). Are Transsexual Brains Different? http://www.mygenes.co.nz/transsexualBrain.htm

Wilkerson, David. (2012) *Have You Felt Like Giving Up Lately? Hope Healing When You Feel Discouraged*. Grand Rapids, MI: Revell.

Made in the USA
Columbia, SC
19 September 2017